In a N ....

by Bob Irving

Eleven Sketches for Church or Conference

No performing rights fee is due for a sketch performed as part of an act of worship, or on an occasion when no admission charge is made, or collection taken to defray expenses. If, however a sketch is performed and an admission charge is made, please write to the publisher for further information.

Published by:
National Christian Education Council
1020 Bristol Road
Selly Oak
Birmingham
B29 6LB

Published for:
RADIUS
Christ Church and Upton Chapel
Kennington Road
London
SE1 7PQ

British Library Cataloguing-in-Publication data:
A catalogue record for this book is available from the British Library.

ISBN 0-7197-0883-4

A co-operative venture in Christian Drama by NCEC and RADIUS.

RADIUS is the shortened name of the Religious Drama Society of Great Britain, bringing together amateur and professional actors, writers, and others involved in religion and the performing arts.

RADIUS exists to encourage all drama which throws light on the human condition, especially through a Christian understanding. It aims to help local congregations towards a deeper appreciation of all types of drama, to inform them of opportunities to see work of a high quality, to give the technical advice and assistance needed for a good standard of local productions, and to help them find ways of introducing the lively arts into their worship.

The society runs a unique lending library, organizes an annual summer school, holds regular play-writing competitions and publishes its own magazine.

First published 1995
© Bob Irving 1995

Typeset by National Christian Education Council
Printed and bound by Street & Co Ltd, Baldock, Hertfordshire.

CONTENTS

THE STORY OF JONAH

Production Note: In casting, Jonah is VOICE 4.
Biblical Background: Jonah 1.1-4.11

VOICE 1	The Reverend Jonah
VOICE 2	Was a famous preacher man.
VOICE 3	A pounder of his pulpit
VOICE 4	As he thundered about sin and judgement and how the wicked would burn for ever in the fiery flames of hell.
VOICE 2	Hot stuff was the Reverend Jonah.
VOICE 1	Then one day he got a message
VOICE 3	From his boss, the Lord above.
VOICE 4	I've got to go to Nineveh, and preach to the people there.
VOICE 2	What an opportunity.
VOICE 3	What a chance.
VOICE 2	They're such terrible, dreadful sinners, you've often said so.
VOICE 3	They'll surely all be condemned, you've often said so.
VOICE 1	The Reverend Jonah didn't look too pleased.
VOICE 4	They're all foreigners. They won't understand. They don't speak English.
VOICE 2	But they'll understand you all right.
VOICE 3	You speak so powerfully. They're sure to understand and to repent.
VOICE 4	Yes, I know, and they will all be saved. God's too soft on sinners, I've often said so. He's too soft on sinners. I didn't get where I am today without knowing that God is too soft on sinners.
VOICES 1, 2, 3	But He's told you to go to Nineveh!
VOICE 4	Yes, I know, I know. So all right, I'm off, I'm off. And I'd be off my head if I went to Nineveh!
VOICE 1	So off he went to Spain.
VOICE 2	The other way.
VOICE 3	Got a last minute, reduced price, standby, no surcharge ticket.
VOICE 2	To the Costa del Fish and Chips
VOICE 3	Where he'd feel really at home.
VOICE 2	He went by sea.
VOICE 3	Why did he go by sea, and not by air?

VOICE 2	'Cos airplanes hadn't been invented.
VOICE 3	I see.
VOICE 2	That's right, by sea is how he went.
VOICE 1	And seeing that the crew were all foreigners, and knowing that you can't trust foreigners,
VOICE 3	And he couldn't trust his stomach,
VOICE 2	He took a large dose of Sea-legs, went to his cabin and fell deeply asleep.
VOICE 1	He went on sleeping while a tremendous, force fifteen-and-a-half gale blew up.
VOICE 2	The Seamen's Union on board
VOICE 3	Decided, by a show of white faces, on immediate panic stations.
VOICE 2	They went to the skipper in a sea-sick body and said:
VOICES 1, 2, 3	Help!
VOICE 1	The skipper said:
VOICE 2	Don't panic. There's a reason for all this. The storm's been sent for a reason.
VOICE 1	The shop steward said:
VOICE 3	It's because of our low pay and terrible conditions of service. And we could bring up the question of food, and we just have brought it all up.
VOICE 2	This storm is not in contravention of previous negotiated settlements. This storm is because of someone on board.
VOICE 3	There are no Militant members in this crew. We're all fully paid-up members of the Party.
VOICE 2	No, no. It's because of that foreign passenger, that foreigner Jonah. I'm sure in my bones it's because of him.
VOICE 1	So they went and woke up Jonah.
VOICE 4	Yes, yes. It is all my fault, let me try to explain and make you understand. You see, my God told me to go to Nineveh.
VOICE 3	Oh, oh, great place Nineveh. We all know about Nineveh. Makes Union Street seem like play school.
VOICE 4	Well, I didn't want to go there, so I decided to go on a holiday in Spain instead. I've been working too hard, you know. Anyway, God is mad at me, and so He sent this storm. All you have to do is chuck me overboard, and it'll all stop.
VOICE 2	We can't do that.
VOICE 3	You may be a foreigner, but we can't do that.
VOICE 2	Wouldn't do that to anyone.

VOICE 1	So the storm continued, and got worse and worse, until eventually with deep regret
VOICE 2	Sorry.
VOICE 3	Sorry.
VOICE 1	They threw Jonah overboard.
VOICE 2	Sorry.
VOICE 3	Sorry.
VOICE 2	Very sorry.
VOICE 3	Very sorry.
VOICE 4	Splash!!
VOICE 1	And up came Jaws Mark 7, opened its huge mouth wide,
VOICE 4	I'd rather not go into that!
VOICE 1	Swallowed him up, and then a day or two later, threw him up,
VOICE 2	Urgh.
VOICE 1	Smelling a bit fishy,
VOICE 3	More urgh.
VOICE 1	On dry land again.
VOICE 2	This time Jonah, having learned of the dangers of being wet,
VOICE 3	Set off to the city of Nineveh.
VOICE 1	To preach to the wicked people there:
VOICE 4	Repent, repent, repent.
VOICES 1, 2, 3	And they did.
VOICE 1	They all repented.
VOICE 2	Every last man, woman and child.
VOICE 3	King and all. They all repented.
VOICE 4	Told you so! Told you so! Told you so! I know what God is like. Now they won't get burned up for being wicked. Too soft on sinners he is. Too soft on foreigners too, if you ask me.
VOICE 1	And Jonah went off and sulked.
VOICE 2	But it was a bit hot in the foreign sun
VOICE 3	And he'd forgotten his sun-tan oil.
VOICE 1	So he sat under the shade of a tree
VOICE 2	And sulked because all the sinners had repented,
VOICE 3	Because all the foreigners had repented.
VOICE 4	They'll be just like us now. Sulk, sulk.
VOICE 1	And he sat there and sulked
VOICE 2	Under the shade of the tree
VOICE 3	Until something strange happened to the tree.
VOICE 2	It got done by leaf drop. All the leaves fell off.

7

VOICE 3	Every last one.
VOICE 1	And there was no shade.
VOICE 2	So Jonah got very hot,
VOICE 3	And very cross,
VOICE 1	And very sorry for the tree.
VOICE 4	Poor tree. It's all that acid rain. The damage we're doing to our environment is terrible. We must save the trees. I'm going to join the Woodland Trust, the Men of Trees, the Save the Rainforests...
VOICE 1	And God said:
VOICE 2	But what about all the people? What about all the people of Nineveh? Aren't you sorry about them?
VOICE 4	They're foreigners. They can't understand. I've got nothing against foreigners, you know. In fact I know some, and really when you do get to know them and understand their funny ways, they can seem almost normal. But it's best if they stay in their own land, in the place you put them, following their own ways. I don't mind them, but we wouldn't want them in our street, now would we?
ALL	*(Looking at audience)* No, we wouldn't, would we?

Talking Point

- What causes racism?
- What do you find most difficult about a different race?

THE SHEEP AND THE GOATS

Biblical Background: Matthew 25.31-46

VOICE 1	Imagine the scene
VOICE 2	Imagine the scene
VOICE 1	At heaven's gate:
VOICE 2	At heaven's gate:
VOICE 1	All sorts of people
VOICE 2	All sorts of people
VOICE 1	Trying to get in
VOICE 2	Trying to get in
VOICE 1	Found themselves divided.
VOICE 2	Really?
VOICE 1	Yes, being sorted out.
VOICE 2	Honestly?
VOICE 1	Different categories.
VOICE 2	Sort of sorting out all sorts of people. Men and women?
VOICE 1	Are there any other sorts?
VOICE 2	Black and white? Old and young? Middle class, working class, social class A1, C3 – that sort of thing?
VOICE 1	Male, female, black, white, all those distinctions don't mean a thing there. There's not that sort of difference.
VOICE 2	What sort of difference is there then?
VOICE 1	Listen.
VOICE 2	I'm listening, sort of.
VOICE 1	You'd better listen real good – that sort of listening. The people who came up all clamouring to be let in had all sorts of reasons for thinking that they should be allowed to enter.
VOICE 2	I can imagine.
VOICE 1	Celia Churchiness said, 'I've been going to my local church every Sunday for the last fifty years. I've not missed a service once unless I was ill or on holiday, and that surely should count for something.'
VOICE 2	I should think it would. Not many people can quote that kind of record. I bet she was let in.
VOICE 1	Nope. Not at all.

VOICE 2	Good grief, why not?
VOICE 1	Listen and you'll learn.
VOICE 2	I hope I will. That sort of thing is just not fair.
VOICE 1	You'll learn. Then there was Fred, the faithful vicar. Been ordained forty years. Improved the services and the hymn-singing no end. Got brand new robes for the choir, faithfully kept all the old traditions going *and* he always agreed with every word the Bishop said! Solid as a rock was Fred.
VOICE 2	He must have got in, that sort of solid citizen.
VOICE 1	He didn't.
VOICE 2	What sort of nonsense is this? It turns everything upside-down! Who else got turned away?
VOICE 1	Harry Hotshot.
VOICE 2	What was *he* like?
VOICE 1	A real whizz. He filled the place every Sunday, filled it with youngsters, backing groups and six guitars, singing super choruses, arms going all about, people waving banners and dancing in the aisles, carrying flags about the place, laying on of hands, praying for the sick...
VOICE 2	He wasn't turned away, surely?
VOICE 1	He certainly was!
VOICE 2	Doesn't make any sort of sense, that doesn't. No sort of sense at all.
VOICE 1	Well you see, he often turns things upside-down.
VOICE 2	Who does?
VOICE 1	The one who stands at the gate.
VOICE 2	Come on, explain why these people weren't allowed in. Tell me just why *good*, religious people, *good*, respectable people, people who attend church as regular as you like, were turned away.
VOICE 1	They wanted to know that as well, and he told them.
VOICE 2	I want to hear this, too right I do. we need to get this sorted. People won't know where they are. Surely going to church and being nice is enough?
VOICE 1	Well, lots of these nice people met Jesus and ignored him.
VOICE 2	How could they possibly ignore *him*? He'd be the one person they would want to meet!
VOICE 1	Remember that old tramp who called at the vicarage and asked for a cup of tea?
VOICE 2	Begging is illegal. It ought to be stopped. You can't have people begging on the streets, it looks so dreadful. We should encourage people to be self-sufficient, not to become layabouts.

VOICE 1	That old man was Jesus.
VOICE 2	Didn't look like Jesus.
VOICE 1	There was the appeal from Africa, asking for aid for the hungry.
VOICE 2	There are so many appeals these days, you get swamped with them. You just can't possibly respond to them all. Anyway, the church roof had to be repaired. Don't tell me one of those Africans was Jesus.
VOICE 1	He was.
VOICE 2	But they were black! Jesus isn't black!
VOICE 1	Then there was the letter from the young man in prison, asking for forgiveness for burgling the pastor's house, and asking the pastor to go and see him in prison.
VOICE 2	That young man is a vicious criminal. He was properly convicted for what he did. You can talk about forgiveness and all that sort of stuff, but he still has to be punished. Prison is the right place for him. You surely aren't going to tell me that he was Jesus?
VOICE 1	That's the strangest of all, strange though it seems, strange though it is, that's what Jesus said. If we visit the prisoners, we visit him!
VOICE 2	I don't believe it.
VOICE 1	He said that those who looked after the hungry and homeless and suffering would go to heaven, even though they didn't realize what they were doing. What mattered was living a life of love, not just going to church.
VOICE 2	Makes you wonder what the point of going to church is. It's meant to make us feel better isn't it? It's meant to make us feel good.
VOICE 1	Jesus says it's meant to make us *do* good, and to start right here and now.
VOICE 2	Right here and now?
VOICE 1	That's what it says. That's what he means.
VOICE 2	There are all sorts of things to sort out, but I can make a start.
BOTH	*(Together to the audience)* So can we all.

Talking Points

- What do you believe happens to those people who do good but who do not believe in Jesus?
- Does believing make us more or less caring?

11

A WOMAN WHO WAS A SINNER

Biblical Background: Luke 7.36-50

VOICE 1	It's a shame.
VOICE 2	A disgrace.
VOICE 1	A wicked waste.
VOICE 2	Simply appalling.
VOICE 3	What she did.
VOICE 2	Never heard the like.
VOICE 1	To begin with,
VOICE 2	That's the proper place to start.
VOICE 3	At the beginning,
VOICE 2	Although there was no end, and no beginning to the way she carries on, from what I've heard.
VOICE 1	Ooh, really? What have you heard?
VOICE 2	That would be telling.
VOICE 3	Go on, tell us then.
VOICE 2	It's not really fit to repeat.
VOICE 1	Well, if it's that bad, I'm sure that i for one wouldn't want to sully my ears by listening to that sort of thing.
VOICE 3	*(Disappointedly)* No, of course not, neither would I. Was it really that bad? Really so bad you can't tell us anything at all about it?
VOICE 2	It was dreadful.
VOICE 1	It must have been awful. *(Pause)* Sure you wouldn't like to tell us about it?
VOICE 3	Now, of course I never want to listen to that sort of thing, but it's obviously affected you very deeply. Maybe it would help you to tell us about it, get it off your chest, sort of thing.
VOICE 2	Talk about sullying your ears by listening to it; I wouldn't sully my lips by talking about it.
VOICE 1	Of course, I blame the television.
VOICES 2 & 3	So do I.
VOICE 1	Did you see that film the other night, on Channel wotsit, you know, the film about You-Know-Who?
VOICES 2 & 3	Oh yes.

12

VOICE 2	Disgusting, wasn't it?
VOICE 3	Appalling.
VOICE 1	Why they make such films, why they have to show that sort of thing, I can't imagine. I mean, what sort of people must watch them?
VOICE 2	Did you not see it then?
VOICE 1	Oh yes, well, it's my husband you know, he will watch all kinds of things, so of course I have to watch it with him. I don't have any choice. Did you see it?
VOICE 3	Well, I'm a firm believer in the power of the OFF switch, turning off the things I don't like, but the same as you, my husband has to keep this sort of thing on.
VOICE 2	What did he think of it?
VOICE 3	Oh, he fell asleep, he usually does.
VOICE 2	So did mine, and I had to watch it alone. Disgusting it was.
VOICE 1	Still, it wasn't as bad as what *she's* supposed to have done.
VOICE 3	No supposing about it. We all know what she's like.
VOICE 2	We certainly do. No doubt about it.
VOICE 1	'Course, I haven't seen it for myself, but everyone says that she's like that, so it must be true.
VOICE 2	No smoke without fire, that's for certain.
VOICE 1	And *he* ought to have known better. Setting himself up to go about doing all these kinds of things, coming out with all kinds of strange ideas. He surely should have known better. It's disgraceful. Makes you lose your faith in human nature, let alone religion. Dreadful.
VOICE 3	It is dreadful, it is. *(Pause)* Who are we talking about?
VOICE 1	You know, him, that fellow from up north who's been going around giving sight to blind people, making lame people walk, curing the sick.
VOICE 2	You must be careful, that's only what people say he does. I've never seen any of it for myself.
VOICE 3	No, you mustn't go just by what people say, you have to have the evidence for yourself.
VOICE 2	I personally, myself, would want to see the cure before my eyes, validated by authentic medical evidence. You can't be too careful. You can't go on hearsay. You have to find things out for yourself, that's what I say. Anyway, what did he do this time?

VOICE 1	Well, it isn't so much what he did as what happened to him – what he let happen to him, come to that. You know he came to town yesterday?
VOICE 3	I didn't know that. I might have thought about going to see him if I'd known. Did you go?
VOICE 1	Yes, I did.
VOICE 2	And what did you think of him? Were you impressed?
VOICE 1	Not a bit. He looked completely ordinary, just like everyone else. Could have done with a haircut, I thought, but then I'm very old-fashioned like that.
VOICE 3	And what happened?
VOICE 1	Nothing then, he was just walking down the street, past the market and through the shopping arcade. It was what happened at night that's set everyone talking.
VOICE 2	What did happen?
VOICE 1	Well, he was invited to dinner with that big shot, Simon the Pharisee.
VOICE 2	Oh, him. Old Toffee-Nose-In-The-Air.
VOICE 3	We know him all right. Got his finger in every pie in this town.
VOICE 2	We know him for sure. I'm told he treats everyone like dirt. I'm glad I've never met him.
VOICES 1 & 3	Me too.
VOICE 2	But we know what sort of man he is.
VOICES 1 & 3	'Course we do.
VOICE 3	We've all heard about him.
VOICE 1	And anyway, this chap, what's-'is-name, he went to dinner with old Simon.
VOICE 2	Who does he think he is? I've never been invited to dinner there.
VOICE 3	Me neither, and even if I was invited, I'm not sure I would want to go. Probably turn it down, I would.
VOICE 1	But he was invited, and while dinner was on, *she* turned up.
VOICES 2 & 3	*She* did?!
VOICE 2	You mean what's-'er-name?
VOICE 3	Thingummy?
VOICE 2	Her what's no better than she ought to be!
VOICE 3	Her what's no better than she is!
VOICES 2 & 3	She turned up?
VOICE 1	Not only did she turn up, she goes straight to the top table, right in the middle of the main course, walks straight up to him, bold as a

14

	brass poker, straight up to him, and takes out the most expensive jar of perfume you have ever seen in your life. Better than anything you could get in the chemist's. Takes the jar, breaks it, *(TWO and THREE shocked tones of 'Aww!')* breaks it, and pours the perfume all over him. All of it. All of it! Can you believe it?
VOICE 3	I can't believe it.
VOICE 2	I not only can't believe it, it's incredible!
VOICE 1	But that's what happened, i tell you. And that's not all. She undoes her hair, bends down and uses it to wipe his feet.
VOICE 3	It's an orgy.
VOICE 2	Disgusting. And what did he do about it? Bet he was shocked, really got his come-uppance.
VOICE 3	A real holy man would have known what she was like, he wouldn't have let her come within a mile of him.
VOICE 1	That's the point see, he was actually, honestly, actually pleased with it all, thanked her, congratulated her and told Simon off for not washing his feet the way she'd done.
VOICE 2	I think it shows him up for what he really is.
VOICE 1	And he went off talking about her needing forgiveness and being forgiven.
VOICE 3	That proves it. Wickedness is wickedness and has to be punished. None of this soft-hearted stuff about forgiveness.
VOICE 2	That's why we've got the crime wave we have.
VOICE 3	Lock up the villains and throw away the key, that's what I say, or at least that's what my husband says.
VOICE 1	Mine does too.
VOICE 2	All this consorting with sinners and forgiving them is not good for us. We have to set firm standards, and stick by them.
VOICE 3	That's what he should have told her. You must change your ways before you come near me.
VOICES 1 & 2	Absolutely.
VOICE 3	By the way, we never did hear exactly what she did do.
VOICE 1	Well, what I heard was this...

All three walk off together gossiping.

Talking Points

- Are there any sorts of people you would rather have nothing to do with?
- Do you know what it feels like to be forgiven?

MOTE AND PLANK

Biblical Background: Matthew 7.3-5

CHAIR   We have called this evening's meeting to consider the very serious problem of traffic congestion in the town and especially in front of the church. You don't need me to tell you how bad it has become. People risk their lives every time they try to cross the road. It takes ages to drive through the town centre. The pollution from vehicle exhausts is getting dangerous, a serious risk to health, and the noise levels are quite atrocious. We can hardly hear ourselves sing in church on Sunday mornings. I have called several expert witnesses to put us in the picture. First of all, Mr Thomas Piper on the question of pollution.

MR PIPER   *(Lights his pipe)* Thanks a lot. We all know how damaging car exhaust fumes are to health. It is quite clear that many cases of asthma, bronchitis, emphysema and other chest diseases are caused by vehicle permissions.

CHAIR   Excuse me, shouldn't that be emissions?

MR PIPER   Quite right, I'm sure. I was saying that all sorts of diseases, not excluding cancer, are probably caused by smoke from exhausts. For our health's sake, we ought to cut down on the amount of traffic.

CHAIR   Can I have a show of hands to indicate our agreement with that? That vehicle pollution is dangerous and ought to be reduced?

> *Pause.*

Thank you very much. That is unanimous. Now, I call upon Mr Decibel to talk about the problem of noise.

MR DECIBEL   The noise situation is, I mean, you know, absolutely sort of diabolical. Sometimes in the mornings when I'm driving to work, I can't hear my car radio at all, and I have to turn it up, you know, full volume so that I can get Radio 1 loud and clear. Know what I mean? Hear what I'm saying?

CHAIR	Very clearly thank you, Mr Decibel. Once again, can I have a show of hands? Do we think that the noise levels are excessive and should be reduced? Thank you. Unanimous again. Thank you, Mr Decibel.
MR DECIBEL	I've not finished yet.
CHAIR	Oh, my apologies, do go on.
MR DECIBEL	And another fing. You get all these people in town in the mornings yeh, what don't know their way about, and you have to keep on blowing your horn to tell them to wake up and get in the right lane. And some of them go so slow you've got to give them a good beep on the hooter to get them moving at all!
CHAIR	I'm not sure how to go about this one. Maybe we could have a show of approval for the idea that people should know where they are going.
MR DECIBEL	Pity we can't all blow our car horns to show we agree.
CHAIR	Yes, but we can't do that, so instead of a show of hands, maybe we could have a good shout to show what we think, clear the lungs, what? Thank you, a most gratifying noise. And thank you, Mr Decibel. Now we come to the problem of traffic congestion. And here we have Mrs Jam to enlighten us, to sort out some of the tangles for us.
MRS JAM	You hardly need me to tell you about the difficulties of congestion in the town. I timed my trip to the library the other morning and it took me all of eight minutes. I'm sure I could have walked it quicker. In a busy, busy life, we need to save all the time we can in all the ways we can. We have so many good works to do.
CHAIR	Don't we all?
MRS JAM	Now, my suggestion for improving the traffic flow in the town is simple. Widen the main road. I know there are all those old buildings there, but it's essential that we don't have to waste time getting to the hypermarket for our shopping. Last week, I was in desperate need of a loaf of bread, and as our local shop has closed down, it took me twenty minutes to get to the big store...
CHAIR	Thank you, Mrs Jam. We all share the difficulty of getting to the stores. She proposes that we support the plan to widen the main road. All those in favour, please show? Unanimous again. Thank you very much. Now, that concludes the business for this evening, so I suggest that we all leave now. As you know, the car park is jammed full with your cars, so we shall need to be a little patient as we leave. Thank you very much.

Talking Points

- How careful should we be in looking at ourselves before we judge others?
- Are there any areas in which you think your church, organisation or group is guilty of looking at the specks of dust in others' eyes and being blind to its own faults?

THE UNJUST STEWARD

Biblical Background: Luke 16.1-8

VOICE 1	This fella...
VOICE 2	Which one?
VOICE 1	You know.
VOICE 2	I don't.
VOICE 1	You must know him.
VOICE 2	I don't.
VOICE 1	Everyone knows him.
VOICE 2	Oh, him!
VOICE 1	That's right, him.
VOICE 2	What's he doing now?
VOICE 1	Not a lot.
VOICE 2	What, him?
VOICE 1	Yes, him.
VOICE 2	*Him?*
VOICE 1	Yes.
VOICE 2	Him, not doing a lot?
VOICE 1	No.
VOICE 2	The original 90s' high-flying, computerized genius, mobile 'phone in every pocket, Porsche in the drive, party every night, new braces every morning, new girl every weekend, top of the dark-suited city sales league, he's not doing a lot?
VOICE 1	No.
VOICE 2	Really?
VOICE 1	Yes.
VOICE 2	What happened?
VOICE 1	He got the push.
VOICE 2	*He* got the push?
VOICE 1	Don't let's start that again. He was sacked, made redundant, got the elbow, given the shove, told to push off.
VOICE 2	Why? What had he done?
VOICE 1	Oh, he hadn't done anything wrong, he'd done everything right, but it was time to reduce overheads, and so, out, head over well-heeled shoes, he went. Bang, goodbye and thank you.

VOICE 2	Just like that?
VOICE 1	Just like that!
VOICE 2	Bet he got a smashing redundancy package though.
VOICE 1	He did, actually, and very clever about it he was too. A real smart, smoothie operation, as you can imagine.
VOICE 2	I can well imagine.
VOICE 1	I bet you can.
VOICE 2	No, actually, I can't imagine, so tell me. What did he do?
VOICE 1	Well, he went to some of the firm's biggest debtors and did a deal with them.
VOICE 2	What sort of a deal? Sounds dodgy.
VOICE 1	It wasn't.
VOICE 2	That was new then. Not like him. What was the deal?
VOICE 1	He knew which outfits were not likely to pay off ever, which ones were going to have to be written off as bad debts, and he said, sort of...
VOICE 2	...Yes?
VOICE 1	Well, sort of, 'cos I don't understand this high finance business too much, he sort of said...
VOICE 2	...Yes?
VOICE 1	'Look, you owe us half a million quid. Now there is about as much chance of your paying it as there is of Torvill and Dean playing rugby for England, isn't there?'
VOICE 2	And then?
VOICE 1	And then he said, 'So let's write down your debt to a quarter of a million and settle for that.'
VOICE 2	And did they?
VOICE 1	They did, handed over their quarter of a million fast as Linford Christie.
VOICE 2	Bet they did.
VOICE 1	And he did that with firm after firm.
VOICE 2	But weren't his bosses annoyed with him for losing all that extra money they were owed?
VOICE 1	No. 'Cos they realized they would only have had to write them all off as bad debts. At least they got something, whereas otherwise they would have got nothing.
VOICE 2	Coo, that was dead smart of him. Nothing like using your head, using all your loaf and going for the main chance, is there?
VOICE 1	That's right, he could see what really mattered, and he went for it.
VOICE 2	And did his firm take him back?

VOICE 1   'Course not. What do you think this is, a fairy story, or some tale from the Bible?

Talking Point

Jesus said, 'Seek first the Kingdom of God'.
● What are the things that prevent you from doing that?
● What can we learn from the world of commerce about being in earnest about our spiritual life?

DRAGNET

Biblical Background: Matthew 13.47-48

VOICE 1	Well, I mean, just look at this old lot here.
VOICE 2	What old lot, where?
VOICE 1	This old lot, here.
VOICE 2	That old lot?
VOICE 1	Yes, that old lot, what did you think I was talking about?
VOICE 2	No idea, I'm sure.
VOICE 1	That's your trouble, no ideas of any sort. Your brain must be a proper jumble sale of a place, full of lots of all sorts of rubbish, and none of it any use.
VOICE 2	Oh, really.
VOICE 1	Yes, really. Now, where was I?
VOICE 2	Standing here. I got that right, didn't I?
VOICE 1	Give me patience! I was talking about this old lot here.
VOICE 2	What old lot, where?
VOICE 1	We're not going on that merry-go-round again. I'm talking about this lot of old junk that they've put on my table.
VOICE 2	But it's a jumble sale, isn't it?
VOICE 1	Of course it's a jumble sale. Anyone can see that for goodness' sake.
VOICE 2	Well, now you've got a lot of jumble that you can sale, I mean sell, haven't you?
VOICE 1	Jumble is what I want; jumble is what the public, the paying public, wants; jumble is what I can sell.
VOICE 2	So now you've got plenty of jumble, haven't you? Lots of things to sell.
VOICE 1	This load of old rubbish isn't jumble, it's just junk.
VOICE 2	How do you mean?
VOICE 1	A pair of wellington boots is what I can always sell. One wellington boot with a hole in it I cannot sell. It's junk.
VOICE 2	Maybe a one-legged fisherman will come along and find that's just what he's looking for.

VOICE 1	Very funny. Here's something else. These days, with all the rage for take-aways, especially Chinese take-aways, you can always sell a pair of chopsticks. One chopstick is no use to anyone.
VOICE 2	Maybe you could use it as a sort of backscratcher!
VOICE 1	And look at this – a pair of saucepans.
VOICE 2	Look very good to me, and that's a good brand name they've got.
VOICE 1	One has no handle and one has a hole in it.
VOICE 2	Could grow geraniums in them.
VOICE 1	That's it, mention flowerpots. I've got sixty-five of them, and every one is cracked.
VOICE 2	Oh dear, you have got a lot of rubbish, haven't you?
VOICE 1	You're beginning to get the point at last.
VOICE 2	But didn't you ask for all this?
VOICE 1	I didn't ask for this lot.
VOICE 2	What lot?
VOICE 1	Now...
VOICE 2	...Sorry, just joking. But you did ask in the church magazine for people to let you have a lot of jumble. Now you've got a lot of jumble, can you really complain?
VOICE 1	I can complain about anything, I've had years of practice at it.
VOICE 2	But isn't there a lot of good, saleable jumble in all that lot that you keep talking a lot about?
VOICE 1	That's a lot of lots.
VOICE 2	Maybe you could auction it off as Lot no. Lot.
VOICE 1	Maybe I could sell a lot of the better pieces. It's not all bad.
VOICE 2	That's life, isn't it. You have to take a lot of the bad with a lot of the good. Not a lot to get worked up about, is there?
VOICE 1	Fat lot you know about it.
VOICE 2	What lot is that?

ONE chases TWO off the stage.

Talking Points

- What do you think the parable of the dragnet tells us about the kingdom of God?
- What in your life causes the most confusion over what is good and what is bad?

IMPORTUNATE WIDOW

Biblical Background: Luke 18.1-8

HOUSEKEEPER	Look here, judge, Your Worship, if I've told you once, I've told you a hundred times.
JUDGE	I should think it's more like a thousand times, and I've told you just as often that I'm not prepared just to put away my stamp collection any old how.
HOUSEKEEPER	That's the whole point, you don't put it away at all. How can I clean your house if you don't at least try to help me a bit? It's like trying to dig the garden with a teaspoon. That room is a disgrace, an absolute disgrace.
JUDGE	Well, to begin with, point one, it is my house, and to go on with, point two...
HOUSEKEEPER	Here we go, just like your summings up in court. Points one, two and three, down to point forty-six and everyone's asleep. Better than counting sheep, you are! Put you on the telly late at night and it would save the NHS a fortune in sedativations.
JUDGE	I sometimes wonder why I put up with this. I am after all, point two, paying you to keep my house clean...
HOUSEKEEPER	Point one, it would be a whole lot easier to keep clean if you were a whole lot tidier, and point two, it would be a whole lot tidier if you were married and not a bachelor, and point three, no wife would put up with all this muddle, and point three, or was it four, or five, or six or whatever, even if you could, and you did get someone, she wouldn't put up with your untidiness, not for a minute. And there must be other points as well, though I can't think of them just for the moment, not being a clever judge like you.
JUDGE	I'm not tidy, I admit it. I'm a paid-up member of that part of the human race which believes that there is a place for everything, and everything in it's place, but I can't ever find the particular place, and I certainly can't find the place to put things in, and then I can't find the things I want to put in that place, so I don't bother to put anything anywhere. Clear?

HOUSEKEEPER	As clear as this place. Pure muddle. I don't know how you got like that. Your mother isn't like it. Look at the fit she had when she last came to stay!
JUDGE	Don't remind me! I nearly sentenced myself to three years in Wormwood Scrubs to get away from it... And how she tidied the place up. She was always meticulously tidy, when I was a child. We had to have a clean bib on at every meal, and woe betide us if we spilled food on the floor or table. She very nearly made us lie at attention in our cots at night. I certainly had to make my toy soldiers stand in line before I went to sleep.
HOUSEKEEPER	Poor thing! So why can't you be like that now? You can't blame it on your mother, she obviously brought you up proper! Why aren't you tidy now?
JUDGE	Because I'm not a little boy any more!
HOUSEKEEPER	How do you get on in court? Do you ever find yourself going into the wrong court room, or sentencing the wrong villain?
JUDGE	I have a clerk who helps to keep me sorted out.
HOUSEKEEPER	Does it ever go wrong? It must do sometimes, if the way you go on at home is anything to go by!
JUDGE	My clerk went off sick once and left me to it. When I got into court, everyone started laughing, and I thought it was because I'd forgotten my wig.
HOUSEKEEPER	And it wasn't? Sure it wasn't because you'd forgotten your trousers?
JUDGE	Partly. I'd put my pullover on my head instead of my wig, and my dressing gown on instead of my robes.
HOUSEKEEPER	I'm not surprised.
JUDGE	But I don't get my stamps mixed up in my collection. They are all kept in proper order. I know exactly what's what there, and usually where it is.
HOUSEKEEPER	Usually, but I have seen you coming out of there all bad-tempered because you can't find some stamp or other. You would help yourself a lot more if you would try, at least try, to keep it all tidy.
JUDGE	I do try, a bit.
HOUSEKEEPER	A very, very little bit. It would help if you let me get in there and sort things out for you. I'd soon put a bit of order into that lot if you would only let me. Only room in the house I'm forbidden to go into.

JUDGE	I don't want you to go in there for the reason which I have told you a thousand times. I don't want all the stamps put away in the wrong places, in the wrong albums.
HOUSEKEEPER	That wouldn't be the end of the world, would it? They're all just stamps aren't they? Little bits of paper that used to be stuck on envelopes.
JUDGE	They're far more than that.
HOUSEKEEPER	Haven't you ever thought of just going out and buying new ones? Don't you ever wonder who has been licking them to put on their letters? Could be harbouring all kinds of horrible tropical diseases: malarimia, choleria and yellow Fred... You could start a buberonic plague in there, you could!
JUDGE	That's utter nonsense, but if you think there are dreadful diseases in my stamp room, isn't that a good reason why you shouldn't go in there?
HOUSEKEEPER	Look, if you aren't afraid to go in, then I'm not. I've had all my vaccinimiations, tentanus and polo and that. All I want to do is go in and clean, just you be a good little judge and tidy your stamps and I'll be in and out in half an hour. Then I promise I won't say another word about it!
JUDGE	You won't?
HOUSEKEEPER	I said I promise. I won't mention it again, if you let me have one good go at it. There. I can't say further than that, can I?
JUDGE	Promise? On oath? You won't say another word about it?
HOUSEKEEPER	Promise, and if I break my word, you can sentence me to three years hard labour, although that'll be nothing new. Plenty of hard labour around here.
JUDGE	Then I promise to tidy up my stamp collection this afternoon. And can I then have a bit of peace? Anything for a bit of peace.
HOUSEKEEPER	Thank you, Your Honour.

Talking Points

- How much effort do you put into your praying?
- Do you really believe that God listens?

THE VINEYARD LABOURERS

Biblical Background: Mark 12.1-9

VOICE 1	'Tis only my due, I say!
VOICE 2	What is only your due?
VOICE 1	Forty years I've farmed this land, man and boy.
VOICE 2	Were you ever a boy?
VOICE 1	'Course I was. Used to fish for sticklebacks in that stream with my jam jar and string. Many's the one I've caught.
VOICE 2	Did you have a fishing licence?
VOICE 1	Don't be ridiculous! Who wants a licence for catching tiddlers?
VOICE 2	Maybe they didn't belong to you.
VOICE 1	Tiddlers, sticklebacks, minnows, they belong to everyone! Nobody owns them.
VOICE 2	Well, you can't catch any now.
VOICE 1	Why not?
VOICE 2	None left. All fished out. Bad as the Spanish fishermen you are!
VOICE 1	Taking things off this land is my due.
VOICE 2	You keep saying that.
VOICE 1	Man and boy...
VOICE 2	*(Interrupting)* Here we go again.
VOICE 1	I've farmed this land all my life. I've looked after it and nurtured it and ploughed it and reaped it, and it's my due.
VOICE 2	Dues again, what's your due?
VOICE 1	To do what I like with this land, and...
VOICE 2	And...
VOICE 1	...And keep the proceeds.
VOICE 2	Keep *all* the proceeds?
VOICE 1	Why not, I've done all the work.
VOICE 2	But you don't own the land, you're only the tenant.
VOICE 1	As good as own it, all the years I've worked it.
VOICE 2	Worked it? You haven't always worked it.
VOICE 1	What do you mean?
VOICE 2	What about the field you say has the biggest cash crop of all.
VOICE 1	Oh, that one.

VOICE 2	Yes, that one, the one that's full of caravans. You don't do a lot of work there.
VOICE 1	Got to collect the money, haven't I?
VOICE 2	What a strenuous occupation!
VOICE 1	I don't know what that means. What I mean is that this is now my land and I should have the money from it as my due.
VOICE 2	Well that'll get you into trouble.
VOICE 1	Let 'em try.
VOICE 2	Didn't I hear that the landlord sent his agent to collect your rent and you sent him off with a flea in his ear? People two farms away could hear you shouting at him. You wouldn't pay him a penny.
VOICE 1	Well, the money wasn't ready. I hadn't put it through the books.
VOICE 2	That's a joke. I didn't know you had any books.
VOICE 1	'Course I have, got to keep the Income Tax man from getting too nosy.
VOICE 2	And didn't the Income Tax man come along and get chased away?
VOICE 1	Maybe he did. I can't help it if my Rottweilers took a dislike to him. Probably didn't like his aftershave. Nothing to do with me. Nothing at all.
VOICE 2	Nothing to do with you?
VOICE 1	Nothing at all, my dogs are working dogs not soft pets. Anyway, he wasn't in hospital long.
VOICE 2	I did hear something about someone else coming along and getting turned away.
VOICE 1	Really?
VOICE 2	Wasn't there someone else?
VOICE 1	Could have been.
VOICE 2	There was, wasn't there?
VOICE 1	Maybe.
VOICE 2	With you, maybe is yes.
VOICE 1	Who did he think he was?
VOICE 2	So there was someone?
VOICE 1	All right, there was.
VOICE 2	Who was he? Another official?
VOICE 1	Not really.
VOICE 2	So who was he?
VOICE 1	He was the landowner's son.
VOICE 2	The landowner's son?

VOICE 1	So he said. 'Course he doesn't really own the land. It's ours because we do all the work on it. If anyone owns the land it's us. This land is ours.
VOICE 2	Isn't it really God's?
VOICE 1	Well, I don't know about that. All I know is that this fellow called himself the landowner's son.
VOICE 2	What did he want?
VOICE 1	Said he wanted to talk to us.
VOICE 2	What's wrong with that? Did you let him?
VOICE 1	'Course not. You know these types, talk you into a corner and out again if you give 'em half a chance.
VOICE 2	And you didn't give him half a chance.
VOICE 1	Not even half. He had an unfortunate series of accidents.
VOICE 2	I bet.
VOICE 1	Broke his ankle in the cattle grid, fell in a pile of you-know-what, ripped his suit on the barbed-wire fence, happened to stand under a bale of straw and got knocked out.
VOICE 2	Terrible.
VOICE 1	It's not. We took him to hospital, all fifteen miles away, on the tractor. We've nothing against him, just that he had what was coming to him.
VOICE 2	But he didn't get what was coming to him. He owned the land, surely that was what should have been coming to him.
VOICE 1	Don't care, it served him right. Coming here, interfering in the way we do things. Trying to tell us how to live our lives. Like I says, it served him right.

Talking Points

- Do we treat the earth as ours, or as belonging to God?
- How will we recognize Jesus when he comes?

ZACCHAEUS

Biblical Background: Luke 19.1-10

VOICE 1	Now in this Bible story, this chap...
VOICE 2	...Yes?
VOICE 1	This chap was a little man.
VOICE 2	A chappette? A mini-chap?
VOICE 1	A little man.
VOICE 2	Really?
VOICE 1	Yes, really.
VOICE 2	You're not just saying that to belittle him?
VOICE 1	No, he was a little man.
VOICE 2	All right.
VOICE 1	So, I'll go on.
VOICE 2	You certainly do go on, telling us over and over again that he was a little man. You haven't told us his name.
VOICE 1	Does it matter?
VOICE 2	Of course it matters, everything matters, it matters a great deal.
VOICE 1	Agreed, so this chap...
VOICE 2	*(Loudly)* ...His name?
VOICE 1	You really want to know?
VOICE 2	I really do.
VOICE 1	Sure?
VOICE 2	I'm sure I'll get mad if you don't tell me his name.
VOICE 1	Zacchaeus.
VOICE 2	Who?
VOICE 1	Zacchaeus.
VOICE 2	That's a name?
VOICE 1	It's a name.
VOICE 2	Sounds like a species of giant spider.
VOICE 1	Some people thought he was more horrible than a spider.
VOICE 2	Not surprised with a name like that.
VOICE 1	His name had nothing to do with it. But people would have nothing to do with him.
VOICE 2	No surprise.
VOICE 1	He was a taxman.

VOICE 2	Even less surprise.
VOICE 1	He worked for the Romans.
VOICE 2	Minus zero surprise! He worked for the occupying forces?
VOICE 1	He did.
VOICE 2	Big deal.
VOICE 1	And he cheated, robbed people high and low, left, right and centre.
VOICE 2	To get a bigger deal.
VOICE 1	Took more than was due in taxes, especially from the poor.
VOICE 2	What a lovely little man.
VOICE 1	So no one would come near him.
VOICE 2	Little wonder.
VOICE 1	But one day, Jesus came to his town.
VOICE 2	And I bet big crowds came out to be near him.
VOICE 1	And little Zacchaeus did too.
VOICE 2	He wanted to see Jesus? *He* did? Cheeky little squirt.
VOICE 1	He really did. But the crowd was too big, and the people were too tall for him to see over, and they gave him a rough time, trod on his feet, pushed and shoved him about.
VOICE 2	Serve him right. Mini menace.
VOICE 1	So he got up into a tree.
VOICE 2	Best place for him. Up a tree.
VOICE 1	Best place to see Jesus.
VOICE 2	Must have been keen.
VOICE 1	Hugely keen he was.
VOICE 2	And did he see Jesus?
VOICE 1	More importantly, Jesus saw him.
VOICE 2	Great! Bet he shrivelled up Zacchaeus with one little look.
VOICE 1	He did look at him, looked straight at him.
VOICE 2	Big moment.
VOICE 1	And Jesus told Zacchaeus to come down.
VOICE 2	Little chance of trying to get away from Jesus.
VOICE 1	He told Zacchaeus he wanted to go to his house.
VOICE 2	To straighten the little twerp out.
VOICE 1	No, to have a meal with him.
VOICE 2	With a big gangster like that?
VOICE 1	With a big crook like that.
VOICE 2	What was the big idea?
VOICE 1	And Zacchaeus came down and said...

VOICE 2	I can guess, 'I'm chuffed to bits, Jesus is coming to my house. I can go on in my old ways. I can become a big man in this little town.'
VOICE 1	A little bit right. He was chuffed to bits, but just being accepted by Jesus made him realize he'd been wrong.
VOICE 2	This is a huge con. I bet he didn't really change.
VOICE 1	Zacchaeus said that he'd pay back four times over anyone he'd cheated.
VOICE 2	Wow! That's a big promise.
VOICE 1	That's right, and that's what he did. He made a huge change in his life.
VOICE 2	That's not just a change in his life. It's an enormous change in the rules. Repent first and then be saved, that's what I thought it had to be.
VOICE 1	Jesus changed the rules. And he changed little Zacchaeus.
VOICE 2	Made him big?
VOICE 1	Made him big-hearted.
VOICE 2	Zacchaeus did change? He really changed?
VOICE 1	He surely did. Jesus can change everyone.
VOICE 2	That's really huge, great, enormous, mega good news!

Talking Points

● Do we have to change to be loved by God?
● Are there any changes you need to make in your life?

THE TEN VIRGINS

Biblical Background: Matthew 25.1-13

VOICE 1	That's half the trouble.
VOICE 2	Not half it isn't.
VOICE 3	What half isn't it?
VOICE 2	One half doesn't know how the other half lives.
VOICE 3	Which half doesn't?
VOICE 1	Both halves doesn't.
VOICE 2	You mean both halves don't.
VOICE 1	You see, that's just what I mean. Half of us trying to communicate and the other half correcting us all the time.
VOICE 2	But half the time you say it wrongly. You use improper grammar.
VOICE 1	I've half a mind to walk off and leave you to it. Then you'd only know half the story.
VOICES 2 & 3	What story?
VOICE 3	You haven't told us any of it yet, let alone half of it.
VOICE 2	Is it a good story?
VOICE 1	Not half it isn't. Like I said.
VOICE 3	So are you going to tell it to us then, or are you going to go off half-cocked?
VOICE 1	Well, all right then. You know the human race is organized into two halves...
VOICE 2	Men and women.
VOICE 1	No, not that, half-wit!
VOICE 3	But one half *are* men and the other half *are* women.
VOICE 1	Yes, but I'm not talking about that. What I mean is that one half of the human race is tidy and organized, and one half isn't.
VOICE 2	I know which half I'm in.
VOICE 3	Me too, can't bear untidiness.
VOICE 2	Better not come round to my place then. My Other Half once put a notice at the door, 'Don't drop any litter in here, you'll never find it again.'
VOICE 1	I always say, you can't have a tidy house and children.
VOICE 2	What's my excuse then?

VOICE 3	But what I say is, 'A place for everything, and everything in its place'. Tidiness is next to godliness, that's what I was taught.
VOICE 2	I expect you've got lists for everything too.
VOICE 3	'Course I have. It's the only sensible way to be.
VOICE 1	What sorts of lists?
VOICE 3	Lists of things I've done, lists of things I've got to do, shopping lists, cleaning lists, gardening lists, job lists, lists of Christmas cards received, lists of Christmas cards to send, lists of people to send holiday postcards to, lists of people not to send holiday postcards to...
VOICE 2	Lists of people *not* to send cards to?
VOICE 3	Yes, they're the ones who don't keep lists themselves, so they'll never notice.
VOICE 2	That's nice. *(Sarcastically)* Very nice.
VOICE 3	And I list words not to use, like nice! I even have lists of my lists.
VOICE 2	Gives you half a mind to throttle people like that!
VOICE 1	But that's what they were like.
VOICES 2 & 3	Who?
VOICE 1	Them. They were members of his fan club. They listened to everything he said on TV or radio. They subscribed to his fan magazine, they read everything they could about him, they absolutely adored him. They even tried to live like him.
VOICE 2	And?
VOICE 3	And?
VOICE 1	One day, they heard he was coming here.
VOICE 2	Here?
VOICE 1	Here.
VOICE 3	So what did they do?
VOICE 1	Worked out the train timetables, learned his route off by heart, decided to invite him to come and meet all the members of the fan club.
VOICE 2	Bet he refused to come.
VOICE 1	You're wrong. He agreed to come.
VOICE 3	That was nice, not half it wasn't.
VOICE 1	But that's not the half of it. They all got ready, and then, disaster...
VOICE 3	...Train was late.
VOICE 2	Helicopter broke down.
VOICE 1	No, don't go jumping in with these half-baked ideas. There were roadworks on the motorway. Disaster. There was a ten-mile tailback.

VOICE 2	That's not a disaster. That's normal.
VOICE 3	So what happened? Did he just go away and not come back?
VOICE 1	No, he kept his promise, and he came just the same, although he didn't come at the time he was expected.
VOICE 2	So they all saw him just the same.
VOICE 1	Not all of them.
VOICE 3	Why?
VOICE 1	Some of them stayed behind, waiting and hoping and making sure that everything was just perfect in case he did turn up.
VOICE 2	And the others?
VOICE 1	Well, they went off down the pub, or home to the telly, or out to the bingo, or down the late-night shops.
VOICE 3	So they missed him?
VOICE 1	Yes! And they weren't half mad!
VOICE 2	They only joined the club because their friends were in it or because it made them feel good. They were in it for their own sakes, so when the time came, they missed him.
VOICE 3	And the others? The other half?
VOICE 1	They were ready, because they were in it for his sake, not theirs. That's how they benefited.
VOICE 2	See what I mean. What matters is being ready, really ready, at any time. Any time.

Talking Points

● Are you ready?
● What can you do to keep really alert spiritually?

DIVES AND LAZARUS

Biblical Background: Luke 16.19-31

VOICE 1	So here we are outside the gates of St Lorramuni in the select and exclusive, indeed private, residential estate of Creditown. We're here for the funeral of Sir Devlin Dividend, one of the biggest names in the area. All the important and influential people for miles around are here, inside the church even as I speak. Just a short while ago, I saw entering the church, Hubert Hubris, Chair of the County Council and member of several important quangos in the district. I also saw Mrs Mildred Manyseats who sits on many of the most prestigious boards in the county.
VOICE 3	*(Dressed very scruffily)* That should be uncomfortable for them.
VOICE 1	Who are you?
VOICE 3	Oh, I'm a friend of Sir Devlin's.
VOICE 1	*(Disbelievingly) You're* a friend of his?
VOICE 3	Well, sort of, in a manner of speaking. He used to give me things, sort of. Gave me a pair of trainers once.
VOICE 1	He did?
VOICE 3	Well, actually I sort of found them in his dustbin. He'd thrown them out, but they were in very good nick. Often found other clothes there too. Sometimes his cook would let me have some grub left over from his dinner parties. Generous old gent, he was.
VOICE 1	You got on well with him?
VOICE 3	Well, yes, in a manner of speaking, or rather not speaking, 'cos he didn't actually talk to me, you know, and I wouldn't expect him to, what with my being homeless and unemployed and all that. But he gave messages through his staff. I shall miss him now he's gone. Miss all his handouts.
VOICE 1	Thank you very much for that warm, human insight into the character of Sir Devlin. That shows another side to the personality of one of the richest men in the neighbourhood. If I can now return to the list of guests at the funeral... There was Boris Banks who has come down from the money markets in the city and from his important work in the Bank of England. Now I have with me an important guest on this occasion, Miss Sarah Stocks, another

member of one of the wealthiest and most important families in the area. Miss Stocks, it seems you've come a little too late for the beginning of the funeral.

VOICE 2   *(Upper class accent)* Yah, yah. It's a frightful nonsense, but you've no idea how hideously busy we've been this morning. It's been utter chaos on all the markets. There's been a shift in the value of the yen and we've been going round in tight Japanese circles trying to sort it out. There's been the chance to make millions and we've put a few more pennies in the bank, I can tell you. Yah, yah. Dear old Devlin would have been on the 'phone to me a few times if he'd still been with us. Sharp eye for a bargain, old Devlin.

Her mobile 'phone rings and she answers it.

Hello. What? What? Of course! Wow! Whoopee! Sell, sell, sell! Now, now, now. Super, super, super! We just can't afford to miss a chance like this.

Replaces the 'phone in her bag.

VOICE 1   Are you not going into the church now, Miss Stocks?
VOICE 3   I don't think I dare. What if the 'phone went again and I had another chance of a bargain like that? I just daren't miss it. Anyway, I know what the funeral will be like. Our vicar's a dear little man, but he will keep going on about God, and it's so mindcrunchingly boring.
VOICE 1   To return to Sir Devlin, how well did you know him?
VOICE 3   Very, very well indeed. Super, super man he was. Devlin wasn't boring you know, he was a lovely man, with a real gift for making money. He used me a lot to advise him on his investments and he just couldn't stop making money. He had the real Midas touch, I'm sure you know what I mean.
VOICE 1   And how did he use his money?
VOICE 2   Well, he did what everyone does these days, he bought a yacht, paintings, holiday homes, a Ferrari, you know, just the usual things.
VOICE 1   He bought a yacht? I hadn't heard that he was a sailor.
VOICE 2   Well, he wasn't really, but he liked to own things. It gave him a real buzz to see his yacht parked in his driveway.
VOICE 1   Well, I see that the congregation are coming out now, so we must move quietly away to let the burial take place.

38

VOICE 2	Oh, yeah.
VOICE 1	And as the crowd of mourners stand in their extremely fashionable mourning clothes, the cortège led by six Rolls Royces draws solemnly away towards the crematorium. And with that, back to the studio.
VOICE 2	Ooh, that was lovely.
VOICE 1	I don't suppose you know anything about his private affairs do you?
VOICE 2	Yes, quite a bit, actually.
VOICE 1	You don't happen to know how much he left, do you?
VOICE 3	I know that.
VOICE 1	You know that?
VOICE 3	'Course I do. It's obvious.
VOICE 1	Obvious? How much did he leave?
VOICE 3	*(Pause)* Everything.

He walks away.

VOICE 1	*(Sardonically)* Oh, thank you very much.
VOICE 2	Who on earth was that weirdo?
VOICE 1	Oh, nobody important.

Talking Points

- Why do we treat rich people as more important than poor people?
- What would you say to a rich person to convince him or her of the importance of spiritual values?

Other Titles from RADIUS and NCEC

THE HILL
Sylvia Read   0-7197-0761-7

A modern mystery play in which the characters find themselves caught up in the experience of Easter. The crucifixion is not just an event of 2,000 years ago, but one of unique importance for today. 45 mins. 7 players

Code No. PLA0761 (A)

CROSSTALK
Bob Irving   0-7197-0795-1

A collection of ten short plays based upon the parables which were, in their own time, sharp contemporary stories in an established tradition. No need for props or costumes, maximum cast of five. Each play lasts about 5 minutes.

Code No. PLA0795(A)

SURPRISE SKETCHES
Ronald Rich   0-7197-0796-X

Five one-act plays with unexpected endings. Each play lasts about 10 minutes. 2-3 players

Code No. PLA0796(A)

THE FLAME
Edmund Banyard   0-7197-0709-9

A novel approach to the idea of Pentecost, this play is a one-act fantasy in the style of the 'Theatre of the Absurd'. Four ordinary people are offered the 'Light of the World' by a messenger from the border between Time and Eternity. 25 mins. 5 players

Code No. FLA0709(A)

A FISTFUL OF FIVERS
Edmund Banyard   0-7197-0667-X

Twelve five-minute plays, each with a Christian message. Using the minimum of actors, scenery and props, these lively sketches will appeal to everyone who is young in the widest sense. 2-9 players

Code No. PLA0667 (A)

A FUNNY THING HAPPENED ON THE WAY TO JERICHO
Tom Long   0-7197-0722-6

The dress rehearsal for a presentation of the Good Samaritan turns out to be more than the leading player intended, as she is challenged by each of the roles she takes on in her search for the one she feels happy with. 30 mins. 5 players

Code No. FUN0722(A)[R]

NATIVITY LETTERS
Nick Warburton   0-7197-0724-2

Highlights the strains put on mother and daughter in the interdependence of a single-parent family, which make them tend to dissociate themselves from other people. Help eventually presents itself through a committed teacher in the daughter's drama group. 40 mins. 5 players

Code No. NAT0724(A)

THE PRODIGAL DAUGHTER
William Fry   0-7197-0668-8

Using a neat twist, William Fry has turned one of the best-known parables into the tale of a present-day girl, updating the setting to portray some of the concerns of modern society. While it shows the seamier side of contemporary life, the message of this play is ultimately one of redemption and love. 30 mins. 11 players

Code No. PLA0668(A)

MORE SURPRISE SKETCHES
Ronald Rich   0-7197-0865-6

Twelve short sketches with a twist in the tail. Ideal as discussion starters on Christian themes. 2-6 players

Code No. PLA0865(A)